The life of Leonardo

Mick Manning and Brita Granström

Illustrated by Brita Granström

OXFORD
UNIVERSITY PRESS

OXFORD
UNIVERSITY PRESS

Great Clarendon Street, Oxford, OX2 6DP, United Kingdom

Oxford University Press is a department of the University of Oxford. It furthers the University's objective of excellence in research, scholarship, and education by publishing worldwide. Oxford is a registered trade mark of Oxford University Press in the UK and in certain other countries

Text © Mick Manning and Brita Granström 2014
Artwork © Brita Granström 2014

The moral rights of the author have been asserted

First published 2014

All rights reserved. No part of this publication may be reproduced, stored in a retrieval system, or transmitted, in any form or by any means, without the prior permission in writing of Oxford University Press, or as expressly permitted by law, by licence or under terms agreed with the appropriate reprographics rights organization. Enquiries concerning reproduction outside the scope of the above should be sent to the Rights Department, Oxford University Press, at the address above.

You must not circulate this work in any other form and you must impose this same condition on any acquirer

British Library Cataloguing in Publication Data
Data available

ISBN: 978-0-19-830824-9

13

Paper used in the production of this book is a natural, recyclable product made from wood grown in sustainable forests. The manufacturing process conforms to the environmental regulations of the country of origin.

Printed in China by Shanghai Offset Printing Products Ltd

Acknowledgments

Series Editor: Nikki Gamble

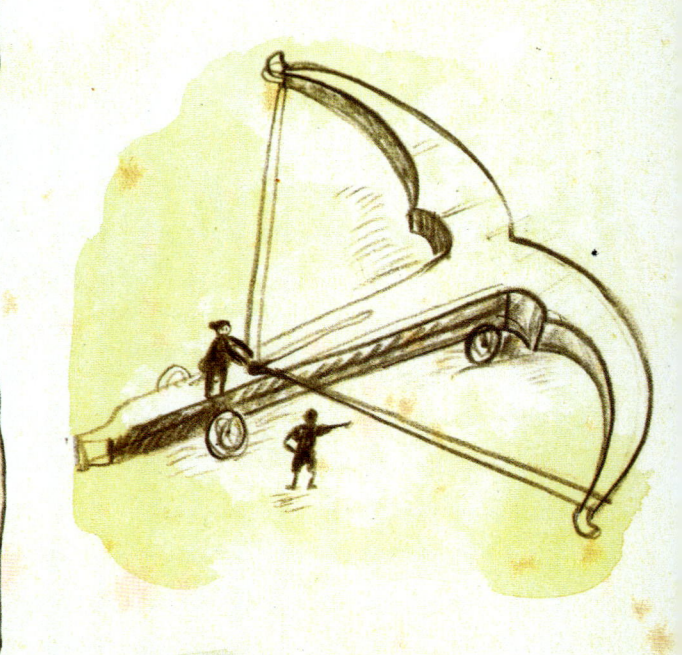

Contents

Me!	4
Training	6
Painter	8
Inventor	10
Flying Machines	12
Weird Writing!	14
The Human Body	16
Machines	18
The *Mona Lisa*	20
My Last Years	22
Glossary and Index	24

Me!

Hello!
I am going to tell you about a genius who lived over 500 years ago – me! My name is Leonardo da Vinci (*say* Lee-oa-nard-oa da Vin-chee) and I was an artist, a scientist and an inventor, too!

I painted some of the world's most famous pictures!

"I amazed people with the fantastic machines I made!"

"My drawings of people helped doctors understand how the human body works!"

"I drew inventions that were too difficult to make until hundreds of years after my death!"

Training

I was born near Florence in Italy in 1452. From a very early age, I wanted to be an artist. When I was a teenager, I went to work for a famous artist in Florence. He taught me how to paint and draw but in return I had to **grind up** his paints and carry his equipment. It was hard work but it made my arms very strong!

"Hurry up and mix me that colour, Leonardo!"

Paints didn't come ready-mixed in those days. The dry colours had to be ground up and mixed by hand. Then egg yolk or oil was added to make paint.

Reddish brown — made from clay

Red — made from the roots of plants or made from squashed beetles

Black — made from burned almond or peach stones

White — made from poisonous lead powder

Painter

In 1472, when I was 20, I began to get my own jobs. I painted **portraits** for rich people, and decorated chapels and churches. But I didn't just want to be an artist! I knew I had to find a job where I could be a scientist and an inventor as well!

I want to be a person who can do everything!

The time Leonardo lived in was known as the Renaissance (*say ru-nai-sons*) — an exciting time of new ideas in **the arts** and sciences across Europe.

Important Renaissance people included:

- the artist Michelangelo, who painted the ceiling of the Sistine Chapel in Rome

- the English author William Shakespeare, who wrote plays including *Macbeth* and *Romeo and Juliet*.

Inventor

In 1482, I wrote a letter to the Duke of Milan, asking for a job. I told him I was a master at inventing new sorts of machines to help with fighting battles. I also said that I could paint whatever he needed me to paint and do whatever he needed me to do! I wasn't showing off — it was all true. After all, I was Leonardo da Vinci!

I can do anything!

The duke was in charge of the area around Milan in Italy. But he wasn't royal, so he really needed to make himself look more important. Paying a great artist like Leonardo to work for him helped the duke show off how rich and clever he was.

As part of his job for the duke, Leonardo organized speeches and discussions. He experimented with science and mathematics — and of course he painted, too.

Flying Machines

By 1485, I was working on a crazy idea – what if I could make humans fly like birds? I made dozens of plans for flying machines, based on my studies of birds' wings. I made over 100 drawings of ways people might fly.

Once you have tried to fly, you will forever walk around looking up at the sky!

There is a story that Leonardo actually built a flying machine and got one of his servants to test it. They say the servant broke his leg when it didn't quite work ...

Sadly, many of Leonardo's ideas never went further than his notebook. So his inventions never actually flew. But modern helicopters are based on his ideas of what he called the ornithopter.

Weird Writing!

I kept notes on my inventions but I wrote them all backwards! This meant they could only be read in a mirror. Some people think I did this to keep my notes secret. Other people think it was because I was left-handed and found it much easier to write from right to left with my feather pen, so as not to smudge the runny ink. What do you think?

Leonardo could actually write and draw using both hands.

"I could write this easily. But it's much easier to read it in a mirror!"

His handwriting was very neat, even if it was backwards!

Can you read this without a mirror? Use one if you need to!

The Human Body

In 1487, I began to study the inside of the human body. The duke allowed me to cut up dead bodies and draw the insides. It might sound horrible, but my drawings helped people, by teaching doctors how the human body works. I used to sing while I worked.

arm

Some people say I am a bit of a show-off. Well, perhaps I am! Besides, look at my amazing drawings!

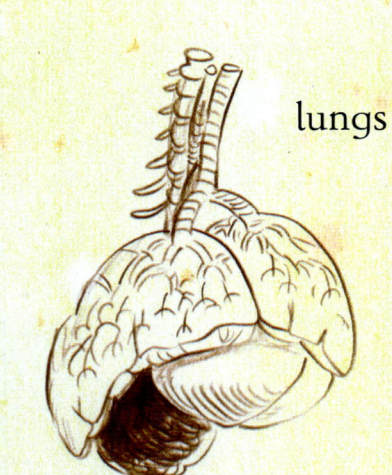

lungs

face muscles

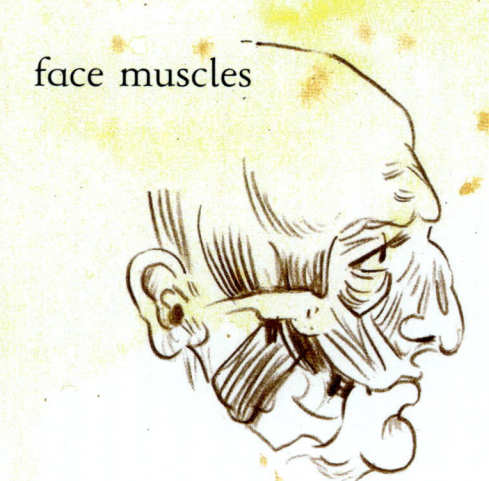

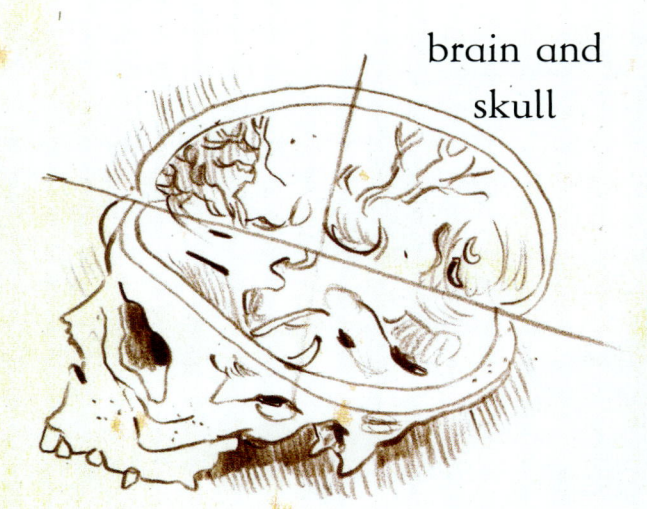

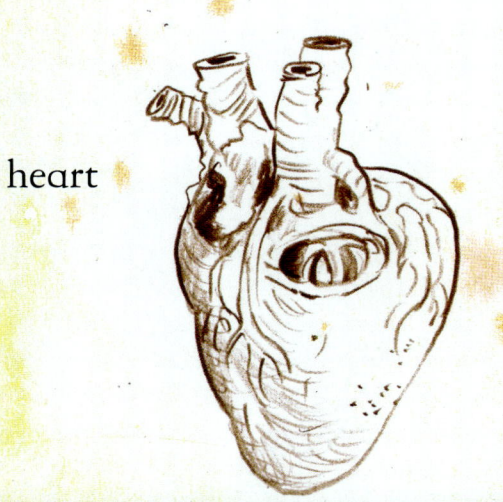

brain and skull

heart

As well as singing, Leonardo played instruments. He even invented a type of musical organ. It was a mixture of a cello and a keyboard ... something like a piano.

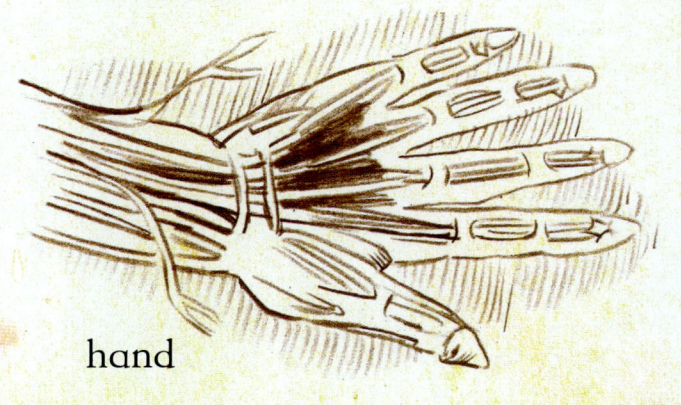

hand

17

Machines

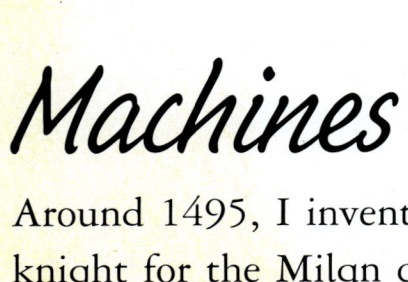

Around 1495, I invented a robot – a **mechanical** knight for the Milan carnival parade! It was made of a suit of armour with ropes, pulleys and wheels inside it to make it move. It could stand up, sit down and even turn its head! It showed the people of Milan just how clever I was!

Look, a mechanical warrior!

My brilliant machines will defeat all your enemies, My Lord!

"Imagine fighting an army of them!"

"I can't believe my eyes!"

giant crossbow

Leonardo drew plans for all sorts of **weapons**. He even designed tanks and submarines, 500 years before anyone else thought of them!

tank

The Mona Lisa

In 1503, I began painting a lovely lady called Lisa. I bet she didn't know that my picture of her would become the most famous portrait in the world!

Leonardo invented a new way of painting, in which shadows and highlights blend together 'like smoke'. He used it to create the *Mona Lisa*'s mysterious smile.

The *Mona Lisa* is **priceless**. It hangs in the Louvre museum in Paris, France.

Another very famous painting by Leonardo is *The Last Supper*. It shows a scene from the Bible and it took him about three years to paint.

My Last Years

In about 1513, I moved to Rome. One day, I made a moving mechanical lion for the King of France. He was so pleased, he invited me to work for him. I lived happily in France from 1517. There was an underground tunnel going from my house to the royal palace.

I was getting old, but I knew my amazing paintings, drawings and inventions would be remembered forever!

In 1519, Leonardo died peacefully in France after a very busy life.

Other amazing inventions found in Leonardo's notebooks include a mechanical cart, **scuba gear**, a **flat-pack** bridge that could be put up anywhere it was needed, and the first ever parachute.

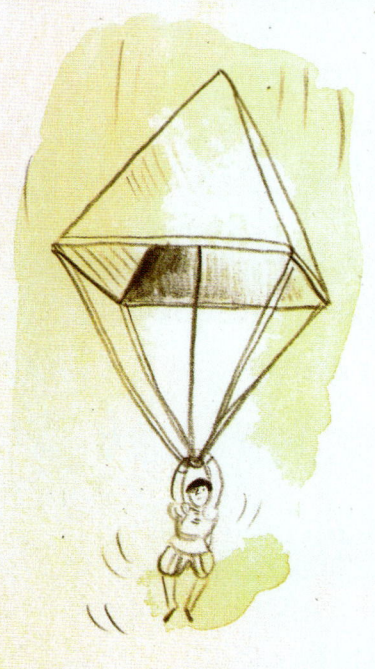

Leonardo's drawings have even helped space scientists develop robots for exploring Mars.

Glossary

flat-pack: packed up flat for moving around

grind up: crush to powder

mechanical: worked by machinery

portraits: pictures of people, often just showing their faces

priceless: very valuable

scuba gear: equipment that divers use to breathe under water

the arts: all kinds of creative work: writing, music, theatre and art

weapons: things used for fighting

Index

artist	4, 6, 8, 9, 11
crossbow	19
flying	12, 13
France	21, 22, 23
helicopters	13
inventor	4, 8, 10–11
Italy	6, 11
left-handed	14
machines	5, 10, 12, 18
Michelangelo	9
mirror	14, 15
paint	6, 7, 10, 21
parachute	23
scientist	4, 8
Shakespeare	9
weapons	19